# DAILY PRAYER PROJECT

ANIMATING A LIFE OF PRAYER THROUGH THE MANIFOLD BEAUTY OF THE CHURCH

## Credits

Unless otherwise indicated, scripture quotations are taken from The Holy Bible, English Standard Version®. Copyright ©2001 by Crossway Bibles, a division of Good News Publishers. Used by permission. All rights reserved.

*All Will Be Well: A Gathering of Healing Prayers,* ed. Lyn Klug. ©1998 Augsburg Fortress.

*Canyon Road: A Book of Prayer* by Kari Kristina Reeves. ©2016 Atlas Spiritual Designs. www.exploreatlas.com. Used by permission.

*I Lie on My Mat and Pray: Prayers by Young Africans* by Fritz Pawelzik. ©1964 Friendship Press.

*Morning, Noon and Night: Prayers and Meditations Mainly from the Third World,* collected and introduced by John Carden. ©1976 Church Missionary Society, London.

*The New Ancient Collects: Completely Revised and Refreshed for Modern Usage.* ©2019 Paul C. Stratman.

"O Ancient Love" by Michael Joncas. ©1994 GIA. All rights reserved. Used with permission.

*Songs of Zion.* ©1981 Abingdon Press.

*With All God's People: The New Ecumenical Prayer Cycle* by John Carden. ©1990 World Council of Churches.

## Staff & Contributors

CO-DIRECTOR
Joel Littlepage

CO-DIRECTOR
Ashley Williams

EDITOR
Russ Whitfield

CURATOR
& COPYEDITOR
Victoria Emily Jones

DESIGNER
Lauren Hofer
Atlas Minor Design Studio

If you would like to receive rights to print and distribute this volume to an organization or congregation, please contact us at team@dailyprayerproject.com to discuss our subscription plan.

The Daily Prayer Project is produced as a ministry of Grace Mosaic in Northeast Washington, DC.

Grace Mosaic is a congregation of the Grace DC Network.

# TABLE OF CONTENTS

**PUERTO RICO**
*Cristian Escobar*

LOCH RAVEN RESERVOIR, MD
*Aaron Burden*

# LETTER FROM THE DIRECTOR

ASHLEY WILLIAMS

"In him was life, and the life was the light of men. The light shines in the darkness, and the darkness has not overcome it."
—John 1:4–5

"Those who look to him are radiant, and their faces shall never be ashamed."
—Psalm 34:5

Merry Christmas and Happy Epiphany to you in the name of Jesus Christ! This Jesus—Prince of Peace and Light unto the nations—has come to you and to me. Behold our King.

Before us, in ages past, others came to behold him. As with any infant brought into this world, the first to behold Jesus was his mother, Mary. Imagine this moment. Mary had been visited by angels with news that she would give birth to the Messiah. In response, likely after many months of pondering and meditating on this news, she burst into song, extolling the promises of God to her people. Deliverance was coming through her womb. That pregnant pause in redemptive history erupted in a manger, and all of creation bore witness to that holy delivery. Beholding her infant's face was to behold salvation and glory. Imagine!

Like family and friends piling into a delivery room, many others would follow quickly after. Among them were three foreigners traveling from east of Palestine to look upon this new King in Jerusalem. A few miles away was a group of shepherds tending to their flock in the weary hours of the night. In the enveloping darkness there burst forth an angel of light with a shout of praise: "Fear not, for behold, I bring you good news of great joy!" These shepherds, like those foreign men, went to behold the newborn Savior. Simeon, a devout one "waiting for the consolation of Israel," beheld Jesus in a temple in Jerusalem. Upon holding him, Simeon broke out into worship with the words with which we end every week: "Lord, now you are letting your servant depart in peace, according to your word; for my eyes have seen your salvation that you have prepared in the presence of all peoples, a light for revelation to the Gentiles, and for the glory to your people Israel."

Friends, our eyes, like these who saw before us, have seen God's salvation through the light and life of Jesus Christ, and the invitation, then, is the same invitation to us today: *Behold!* But what does it mean to behold? It certainly means to look, but it is much more than that. The word's etymology suggests more than a cursory glance or even an intent look; it is a considering, a possessing, and of course, a holding. It is to keep and preserve that which was seen so that one's life is transformed by the sight. Our hope as we've curated the Christmas and Epiphany edition is that we would aid your looking at this King, for to look is to live.

We are guided to behold in various ways throughout this edition. We've included eight Nativity artworks from various countries, like a painting by Japanese artist Hiroshi Tabata and a linocut by Azaria Mbatha of South Africa. These visuals are helpful objects for Susan Porterfield Currie's encouragement toward holy gazing using the ancient practice of *visio divina*. Our readings and prayers provide fodder for meditation, an act that Russ Whitfield compares to eating—a holy feasting on God's word, and work for spiritual nourishment and renewal. These elements and more have been curated with one solitary objective in mind: to behold our God.

There is so much in our world to behold. Especially in this season of Christmas and Epiphany, distractions and hurry often abound. Our hope for you is that amid all the sparkly lights and festive decorations, you'd be reminded to slow down, to behold, and to pray without ceasing.

# INTRODUCTION

The Daily Prayer Project (DPP) is a movement that exists to animate the life of prayer through the manifold beauty of the church. We connect and unify Christians by resourcing them with daily prayers, practices, and music from the global-historical church, and visual art of spiritual and artistic value. All of these rich resources are crafted into a simple, functional, and beautiful product: our Living Prayer Periodicals (LPPs). This is what you are holding in your hands right now.

We produce six LPP editions per year that move with the Christian seasons of Advent, Christmas & Epiphany, Lent, Easter, Pentecost, and Ordinary Time. These editions combine dynamic and diverse content with a stable method for morning and evening prayer.

This method not only provides consistency for the life of prayer and practice, but it also forms us all into a life of communion with God and unity with our global and historical family of faith. It is this communal prayer that fuels and forms our own expressions of prayer in the present season of our lives. The DPP is an entrance into the holy, unifying, and empowering experience of praying together in a common way without ceasing throughout the Christian year.

The Daily Prayer Project logo is a monogram crafted into a prayer labyrinth. The mark itself becomes a practice of prayer. Rooted in the ancient Christian tradition of pilgrimage, prayer labyrinths have a history as far back as the fourth century in an Algerian church.

A labyrinth is not a maze. There is one entry point, and a single pathway leading to the center. The journey is a transformative walk toward God, the center of the labyrinth. Arriving at the center symbolizes union with God. Once a pilgrim has this encounter, they are led back out into the world along the same path.

Walking a labyrinth is a slow, meditative practice. This is a way to embody your prayer. The mark is placed above for you to travel the path of the labyrinth with your finger as a small gesture of this larger practice. We hope that one day you might be able to encounter God as you walk through a physical prayer labyrinth.

# Daily Prayer Project Lectionary

A lectionary is a schedule of Bible readings that is meant to help Christians read the whole Bible over a period of time, emphasizing particular themes and narratives during particular seasons of the Christian year. The Daily Prayer Project follows the Sunday (and certain holy day) readings of the Revised Common Lectionary, the largest shared Bible-reading plan in North America. For most Monday–Saturdays, we follow our own Daily Prayer Project Lectionary, which moves through scripture in a slow, three-year cycle. The DPP Lectionary is broken down into three categories of readings from scripture: the Psalms, the Old Testament, and the New Testament. The Old Testament is broken down into its traditional three parts: (1) Law & History, (2) Wisdom & Poetic Literature, and (3) the Prophets. The New Testament is also broken down into its traditional three sections: (1) the Four Gospels & Acts, (2) the Pauline Epistles, and (3) the General Epistles. Lectionaries are a time-tested tool from the history of the church for maintaining a steady "diet" from the Bible's different parts. They are specifically designed to lighten the daily load of reading and to help the reader focus in on smaller passages and particular books at a time. This facilitates slower, more meditative reading. Currently, the DPP is in Year B of the lectionary.

|  | YEAR A | YEAR B | YEAR C |
|---|---|---|---|
| **The Psalms** | ALL 150 PSALMS <br> 2x/Year | ALL 150 PSALMS <br> 2x/Year | ALL 150 PSALMS <br> 2x/Year |
| **Old Testament** | LAW & HISTORY <br> Genesis–Leviticus | LAW & HISTORY <br> Numbers–2 Samuel | LAW & HISTORY <br> 1 Kings–Esther |
|  | WISDOM & POETRY <br> Proverbs & Job | WISDOM & POETRY <br> Proverbs & Ecclesiastes | WISDOM & POETRY <br> Proverbs & Song of Songs |
|  | PROPHETS <br> Isaiah <br> & Minor Prophets (Part I) | PROPHETS <br> Jeremiah, Lamentations <br> & Minor Prophets (Part II) | PROPHETS <br> Ezekiel <br> & Minor Prophets (Part III) |
| **New Testament** | GOSPEL & ACTS <br> Matthew, Mark & Acts | GOSPEL & ACTS <br> Luke & Acts | GOSPEL & ACTS <br> John & Acts |
|  | PAULINE EPISTLES <br> Romans–Titus | PAULINE EPISTLES <br> Romans–Titus | PAULINE EPISTLES <br> Romans–Titus |
|  | GENERAL EPISTLES <br> Hebrews–Revelation | GENERAL EPISTLES <br> Hebrews–Revelation | GENERAL EPISTLES <br> Hebrews–Revelation |

*Sundays and holy days are from the Revised Common Lectionary*

## Methods & Elements

Each day of the LPP features morning and evening prayer liturgies framed by seven core elements. Everyone's style of praying is different because every person is different. Beyond that, Christian prayer varies widely across cultures and denominations. No single method can capture this. However, we hope you find within the LPP a rhythm that gives enough structure and freedom to facilitate a diverse community of prayer. Every element is offered as a guiding movement, not as a binding rule. You are encouraged to modify the liturgy based on the context of prayer. Consider establishing rhythms of prayer in your congregation, household, workplace, small groups, or other gatherings so that you might experience the formative reality of common prayer. If doing this liturgy individually, you are encouraged to take your time to soak it in. If doing it as a group, it may be best to alternate leading each element. Also, consider using different postures in prayer (standing, kneeling, lifted or open hands, lying prostrate, etc.) that fit your context.

CALL: There is an invitation always open to us. The Spirit of God calls us to come into the holy presence, and we respond to this welcome by entering in.

PSALM: The Psalms form the core language of prayer for the people of God and have done so for thousands of years. The Psalms give us language and postures of heart and body to express in the presence of God.

ADORATION: We were created to adore God, and in the place of worship we find the joy of this purpose. This adoration happens in both silence and song. We provide three to four songs per edition in the Songbook found on pages 53–57. Full recordings and resources for these songs and others can be found at dailyprayerproject.com. You are also encouraged to sing songs from your own community.

LESSON: The scriptures give us the story of the Father's redemption of all things in the Son by the power of the Holy Spirit.

PRAYER: We are led across praise, confession, and guided intercessory prayer by our family of faith all over the globe and throughout time. We receive every prayer as a gift as we put them on our own lips and in our own hearts. These prayers range from traditional prayers of the universal church to more modern and meditative prayers.

ABIDING: In response to what we have encountered in the first five elements, Abiding is an opportunity for deeper communion and self-reflection through meditating on the scriptures (*lectio divina*), considering the art in the gallery (*visio divina*), or using our bodies to engage historical Christian practices (*praxio divina*). Out of that place, we are also prompted to pray for the needs of others in different stations of life.

BENEDICTION: We close our time with a word of love and blessing over our lives from God himself, the Alpha and the Omega, the Beginning and the End. Our journey of prayer is framed by the Call and the Benediction; God has the first and the last word over all things in our lives.

Nathan Dumlao

## Adapting the LPP for Household Prayer

*A Five-Element Method*

We have often been asked how to adapt the Living Prayer Periodicals for household prayer, especially when that involves small children. It is an important question and one that we want to provide some suggestions for in this Advent edition. These suggestions come after years of practice and experimenting within our own communities and families. The liturgies can be practiced once or twice a day, depending on your household rhythms. In my house, we practice communal prayer around the table once we finish dinner (almost!) every evening.

Disclaimer: If you have small children, prayer time will probably not always be peaceful and beautiful. These times might involve some chaos, disordered noise, fighting, arguing, silly laughter, etc. That's OK! Especially as children begin developing new habits and growing in their ability to pay attention, you are encouraged to let them grow in this way and to take your time growing in prayer together. There is no hurry, and things need not be perfect. The Lord is with you and your family and merely desires your presence. The important part is finding a simple rhythm and sticking to it because children (and adults) thrive on rhythms.

The following suggested method takes the seven core elements of the LPP liturgies and reduces them to five:

CALL
LESSON (Psalm, OT, or NT)
ABIDING
THE LORD'S PRAYER
BENEDICTION

Here are some practical suggestions for implementing this method:

- Before you begin to pray together, select what your Lesson reading is going to be. For example, if the scripture readings that day are Psalm 62, Leviticus 12, and Mark 10, then choose one or a section of one of those to attend to. It will probably be best for those with small children to begin small. If Mark 10 is chosen, then choose just one of the sections of that chapter.
- Before you begin to pray together, distribute the parts of the liturgy to different members of the household. In my household we have five people, so each member is responsible for one movement of the liturgy. If you have children who can read, they might relish the chance to read a different part each day. We keep a chart on the wall with the day, the five elements, and the person's name, giving each person a chance to do different parts throughout the week.
- If children cannot read, worry not! Children also love to do call-and-response, and this is how their language is formed. For my youngest son, who cannot read, his mother or I whisper the words of the call in his ear and he then gets to say them loudly for the family prayer time. He loves it, and yes, it is often adorable.
- Begin each time of prayer by taking some breaths together as a family (we often do three deep breaths), bringing stillness to your bodies, hearts, and minds.
- CALL: Again, children often love call-and-response! If necessary, teach them what their response line is going to be (the words in bold). Then someone should read the call and hear the response of the rest of the table.
- LESSON: Read the passage of scripture you selected before, or have one of the children read it (mine fight over this privilege . . .).
- ABIDING: This element can be really flexible as far as what is done and how long it takes. Here is a suggested flow:

1. You might begin by actually reading the italicized text in the Abiding section: "Pause at the start/end of this day. Enjoy communion with the living God . . ." Or maybe start this time by singing a song together (e.g., a song from the back of the book or one from your church's worship service).
2. Then invite some reflection on the scripture reading you just heard together by asking simple questions: "What did you hear in that passage?" "What stuck out to you?" "What did Jesus do?" "What do you think it meant when it said _____?" You might get asked a question that you don't know the answer to, and that's perfectly fine! We are all always learning together.
3. From here you could pray one of the provided prayers in the LPP for that day, you could pray using one or more of the prompts, you could pray as the passage you heard leads you, or you could practice intercessory prayer.

- THE LORD'S PRAYER: Simply pray this together every day as Jesus taught us.
- BENEDICTION (feel free to call it a "blessing" or "God's good word"): When we practice this element, the person giving the benediction raises their hands and puts them outward while the rest around the table open their hands, palms up, in a posture of reception. Then the benediction is spoken and the time of prayer comes to an end.

This is merely a suggested method, and you are encouraged to modify, reduce, or expand it as fits the context of your household. Our prayer is that you can find your communal rhythm of communing with the Creator and experience the beauty and shalom that comes from praying together.

Let us pray,
*Joel Littlepage*

## Seasons of the Christian Year

At the Daily Prayer Project we practice the global and historical tradition of the Christian year (sometimes called the liturgical year or church year) as a communal rhythm that forms us—year after year, season after season—to be the people of God and the bearers of God's story. Human beings are creatures fundamentally and profoundly shaped by stories. Each of our lives will always be following someone's calendar and bearing someone's story, but the question is: whose story is it, and what kind of narrative it is telling? The Christian year is an ancient Christian tradition of ordering the 365-day calendar year around the life of Christ. Some dates and celebrations vary by Eastern and Western Christian traditions, but they are generally as follows: Advent,

Christmastide, Epiphany (also called Ordinary Time in some traditions), Lent, Eastertide, and Ordinary Time.

The Daily Prayer Project crafts each edition of the LPP in accordance with the Christian year, with six editions per annual cycle. Most editions average eight weeks, except the Ordinary Time edition, which spans about sixteen weeks in the fall. Christmas and Epiphany (with Epiphanytide extending through the eve of Ash Wednesday) are combined into a single edition, and we celebrate the season of Pentecost for eight weeks, from the day of Pentecost to the eve of the eighth Sunday of Ordinary Time. Each season has been assigned a liturgical color and seasonal icon.

**CHRISTMAS & EPIPHANY** | DECEMBER 25, 2022–FEBRUARY 21, 2021

The season of Christmas (also known as Christmastide) begins on December 25 and stretches twelve days until the Epiphany of our Lord on January 6. This ancient rhythm is one of feasting, generosity, and joy that celebrates the unparalleled gift of the incarnate Son of God. Epiphany, a word that means "manifestation," is a day and season that celebrates the revelation of Jesus to all nations and peoples. On Epiphany the church remembers the visit of the magi from the East as well as the baptism of Jesus.

## 2022–2023 Christian Year

**ADVENT**

Nov 27–Dec 24

**CHRISTMAS & EPIPHANY**

Dec 25–Feb 21

**LENT**

Feb 22–Apr 8

**EASTER**

Apr 9–May 27

**PENTECOST**

May 28

**ORDINARY TIME**

May 29–Dec 2

PRAYERS
SUNDAY MORNING TO WEDNESDAY EVENING

WATERTOWN, MA
*Osman Rana*

# SUNDAY

## Call

Blessed be the Lord God of Israel, **for he has visited and redeemed his people.**

*Luke 1:68*

## Psalm

*Read the Psalm of the day.*

### GLORIA IN EXCELSIS DEO

Glory to God in the highest and peace to his people on earth. Lord God, heavenly King, Almighty God and Father, we worship you, we give you thanks, we praise you for your glory. For you alone are the Holy One, you alone are the Lord, you alone are the Most High, Jesus Christ, with the Holy Spirit, in the glory of God the Father. Amen.

## Adoration

### SILENCE OR SONG

*Seasonal song selections can be found on pp. 53–57.*

## Lesson

*Read the New Testament passage of the day.*

## Prayer

O ancient love, processing through the ages:
O hidden love, revealed in human form:
O promised love, the dream of seers and sages:
**O living Love, within our hearts be born.**
O homeless love, that dwells among the stranger:
O lowly love, that knows the mighty's scorn:
O hungry love, that lay within a manger:
**O living Love, within our hearts be born.**
O gentle love, caressing those in sorrow:
O tender love, that comforts those forlorn:
O hopeful love, that promises tomorrow:
**O living Love, within our hearts be born.**

**DEC 25**
*Christmas Day*
ISA. 52:7-10
PS. 98
JOHN 1:1-14; TITUS 3:4-7

**JAN 1**
ISA. 63:7-9
PS. 148
MATT. 2:13-23;
HEB. 2:10-18

**JAN 8**
ISA. 42:1-9
PS. 29
MATT. 3:13-17;
ACTS 10:34-43

**JAN 15**
ISA. 49:1-7
PS. 40
JOHN 1:29-42;
1 COR. 1:1-9

**JAN 22**
ISA. 9:1-4
PS. 27
MATT. 4:12-23;
1 COR. 1:10-18

O suff'ring love, that bears our human weakness:
O boundless love, that rises with the morn:
O mighty love, concealed in infant meekness:
**O living Love, within our hearts be born.**

Adapted from the hymn "O Ancient Love" by Michael Joncas

## Abiding

LECTIO DIVINA, VISIO DIVINA, OR PRAXIO DIVINA

*Pause at the start of a new day. Enjoy communion with the living God: Father, Son, and Holy Spirit. Listen for the voice of God in the scriptures. Read. Meditate. Pray. Contemplate. Seek God's face.*

### PROMPTED PRAYER

- For a wonder at the incarnation of the Lord Jesus
- For those who come into worship feeling a great curiosity about the Christian faith
- For those who worship under the threat of persecution today

### THE LORD'S PRAYER

Our Father who art in heaven, hallowed be thy name. Thy kingdom come, thy will be done, on earth as it is in heaven. Give us this day our daily bread; and forgive us our debts, as we forgive our debtors; And lead us not into temptation, but deliver us from evil. For thine is the kingdom and the power and the glory, forever. Amen.

## Benediction

Hear the Lord Jesus say: "I am the Alpha and the Omega, the first and the last, the beginning and the end. I am the root and the descendant of David, the bright morning star." May the Bright Morning Star shine upon you today

*Adapted from Revelation 22:13, 16*

## Call

Those who dwell at the ends of the earth are in awe at your signs. **You make the going out of the morning and the evening to shout for joy.**

*Psalm 65:8*

## Psalm

*Read the Psalm of the day.*

### GLORIA IN EXCELSIS DEO

Glory to God in the highest and peace to his people on earth. Lord God, heavenly King, Almighty God and Father, we worship you, we give you thanks, we praise you for your glory. For you alone are the Holy One, you alone are the Lord, you alone are the Most High, Jesus Christ, with the Holy Spirit, in the glory of God the Father. Amen.

## Adoration

### SILENCE OR SONG

*Seasonal song selections can be found on pp. 53–57.*

## Lesson

*Read the Old Testament passage of the day.*

## Prayer

The Evil One knew how to harm us, and by lights he blinded us— by possessions he hurt us, through gold he made us poor— by the graver's graven images, he made us a heart of stone. Blessed is he who came and softened it! Sin had spread its wings and covered all things, that none could discern, of himself or from above, the truth.

Truth came down into the womb, came forth, and rolled away error. Blessed is he who dispelled sin by his birth! Unveil and make glad your face, O creature, in our feast. Let the church sing with voice; heaven and earth, in silence! Sing and praise the Child, who has brought release for all! Blessed be he who has loosed the bonds! Amen!

*A prayer of Ephrem the Syrian (306–373 CE), taken from his Hymns on the Nativity, no. 15*

## Abiding

### LECTIO DIVINA, VISIO DIVINA, OR PRAXIO DIVINA

*Pause at the end of this day. Enjoy communion with the living God: Father, Son, and Holy Spirit. Listen for the voice of God in the scriptures. Read. Meditate. Pray. Contemplate. Seek God's face.*

### INTERCESSORY PRAYER

Pray for the known needs of your church, neighborhood, city, and world.

## Benediction

And I heard a loud voice from the throne saying, "Behold, the dwelling place of God is with man. He will dwell with them, and they will be his people, and God himself will be with them as their God." May you rest in this eternal promise of a dwelling place with God.

*Adapted from Revelation 21:3*

**JAN 29**

MIC. 6:1-8

PS. 15

MATT. 5:1-12;

1 COR. 1:18-31

**FEB 5**

ISA. 58:1-12

PS. 112

MATT. 5:13-20;

1 COR. 2:1-16

**FEB 12**

DEUT. 30:15-20

PS. 119

MATT. 5:21-37;

1 COR. 3:1-9

**FEB 19**

EXOD. 24:12-18

PS. 2

MATT. 17:1-9;

2 PET. 1:16-21

EVENING PRAYER

# MONDAY

MORNING PRAYER

## Call

Oh sing to the LORD a new song,
**for he has done marvelous things!**

*Psalm 98:1*

## Psalm

*Read the Psalm of the day.*

### GLORIA IN EXCELSIS DEO

Glory to God in the highest and
peace to his people on earth.
Lord God, heavenly King,
Almighty God and Father,
we worship you, we give you thanks,
we praise you for your glory.
For you alone are the Holy One, you alone
are the Lord, you alone are the Most High,
Jesus Christ, with the Holy Spirit, in
the glory of God the Father. Amen.

## Adoration

### SILENCE OR SONG

*Seasonal song selections can be found on pp. 53–57.*

## Lesson

*Read the Old Testament passage of the day.*

## Prayer

Wonderful, merciful God,
I put myself in your hands with the first
breath this morning.
I know you are alive.
I know your goodness and grace have no end.
I beg you, heavenly Father,
take my day into your hands.
Push away all the temptations and wants of
this day,
as you push away threatening storm clouds.
Let me do my work,
let me do it so that it is good for my
neighbors and glorifies your name.

Give me right words and power and love,
so that your image may be rightly painted for
my neighbors.
May my work be fruitful.
Amen.

A prayer of a young Christian in Ghana, taken from *I Lie on
My Mat and Pray*

## Abiding

### LECTIO DIVINA, VISIO DIVINA, OR PRAXIO DIVINA

*Pause at the start of a new day. Enjoy communion with the living
God: Father, Son, and Holy Spirit. Listen for the voice of God in
the scriptures. Read. Meditate. Pray. Contemplate. Seek God's face.*

### PROMPTED PRAYER

- For gratitude for God's grace to us
  in the gift of the Messiah Jesus
- For humility, patience, and hope to
  imagine new patterns in this new year
- For immigrants and refugees and
  those who minister to them

### THE LORD'S PRAYER

Our Father who art in heaven, hallowed
be thy name. Thy kingdom come, thy
will be done, on earth as it is in heaven.
Give us this day our daily bread; and forgive
us our debts, as we forgive our debtors;
And lead us not into temptation,
but deliver us from evil.
For thine is the kingdom and the
power and the glory, forever. Amen.

## Benediction

In him was life, and the life was the light of
men. The light shines in the darkness, and
the darkness has not overcome it. May you
walk forward in this unconquerable light!

*Adapted from John 1:1–5*

## Call

"Lord, to whom shall we go?
**You have the words of eternal life."**

*John 6:68*

## Psalm

*Read the Psalm of the day.*

### GLORIA IN EXCELSIS DEO

Glory to God in the highest and
peace to his people on earth.
Lord God, heavenly King,
Almighty God and Father,
we worship you, we give you thanks,
we praise you for your glory.
For you alone are the Holy One, you alone
are the Lord, you alone are the Most High,
Jesus Christ, with the Holy Spirit, in
the glory of God the Father. Amen.

## Adoration

### SILENCE OR SONG

*Seasonal song selections can be found on pp. 53–57.*

## Lesson

*Read the New Testament passage of the day.*

## Prayer

**Confession:** Give me a clean heart so
I may serve Thee. Lord, fix my heart
so that I may be used by Thee. For I'm
not worthy of all these blessings. Give
me a clean heart, and I'll follow Thee.

Adapted from the song "Give Me a Clean Heart" by Margaret
Pleasant Douroux (1941–), taken from *Songs of Zion.* Ms.
Douroux is an American gospel songwriter, teacher, and author.

**Assurance:** But when the fullness of
time had come, God sent forth his Son,
born of woman, born under the law, to
redeem those who were under the law,
so that we might receive adoption as
sons. And because you are sons, God
has sent the Spirit of his Son into our
hearts, crying, "Abba! Father!" So you
are no longer a slave, but a son, and if
a son, then an heir through God.

*Galatians 4:4–7*

## Abiding

### LECTIO DIVINA, VISIO DIVINA, OR PRAXIO DIVINA

*Pause at the end of this day. Enjoy communion with the living God:
Father, Son, and Holy Spirit. Listen for the voice of God in the
scriptures. Read. Meditate. Pray. Contemplate. Seek God's face.*

### INTERCESSORY PRAYER

Pray for the known needs of your
church, neighborhood, city, and world.

## Benediction

The LORD has made known his salvation;
he has revealed his righteousness in the
sight of the nations. He has remembered
his steadfast love and faithfulness to
the house of Israel. May his steadfast
love be upon us as we hope in him.

*Adapted from Psalm 98:2–3*

| | |
|---|---|
| **JAN 30** | NUM. 20 |
| | PS. 43 |
| | LUKE 3:1-20 |
| **FEB 6** | NUM. 26 |
| | PS. 49 |
| | LUKE 5:17-26 |
| **FEB 13** | NUM. 32 |
| | PS. 55 |
| | LUKE 7:1-10 |
| **FEB 20** | DEUT. 2 |
| | PS. 61 |
| | LUKE 8:22-39 |

EVENING PRAYER

# TUESDAY

## Call

Arise, shine, for your light has come,
**and the glory of the LORD
has risen upon you.**

*Isaiah 60:1*

## Psalm

*Read the Psalm of the day.*

### GLORIA IN EXCELSIS DEO

Glory to God in the highest and
peace to his people on earth.
Lord God, heavenly King,
Almighty God and Father,
we worship you, we give you thanks,
we praise you for your glory.
For you alone are the Holy One, you alone
are the Lord, you alone are the Most High,
Jesus Christ, with the Holy Spirit, in
the glory of God the Father. Amen.

## Adoration

### SILENCE OR SONG

*Seasonal song selections can be found on pp. 53–57.*

## Lesson

*Read the New Testament passage of the day.*

## Prayer

Merciful and most loving God, by your
will and mercy Jesus Christ our Lord
humbled himself to exalt all humanity,
and descended to the depths to lift up
the lowly, and was born of a virgin, fully
God and fully human, to restore in us your
holy image that had been lost. Grant that
your people may cling to you, that as you
have redeemed us in your mercy, we may
always please you by devoted service.

An ancient prayer taken from the Gallican Rite, a Latin Christian liturgy translated from the Syriac-Greek rites of Jerusalem and Antioch in the early centuries of the church. Taken from *The New Ancient Collects.*

## Abiding

### LECTIO DIVINA, VISIO DIVINA, OR PRAXIO DIVINA

*Pause at the start of a new day. Enjoy communion with the living God: Father, Son, and Holy Spirit. Listen for the voice of God in the scriptures. Read. Meditate. Pray. Contemplate. Seek God's face.*

### PROMPTED PRAYER

- For the ability to see our own deficiencies and know the sufficiency of Jesus
- For the faithful witness of the church in your city and country
- For the poor and oppressed in your city

### THE LORD'S PRAYER

Our Father who art in heaven, hallowed
be thy name. Thy kingdom come, thy
will be done, on earth as it is in heaven.
Give us this day our daily bread; and forgive
us our debts, as we forgive our debtors;
And lead us not into temptation,
but deliver us from evil.
For thine is the kingdom and the
power and the glory, forever. Amen.

## Benediction

Hear the Lord say, "I am the light
of the world. Whoever follows
me will not walk in darkness,
but will have the light of life." May
you go from this place following
after the Light of the World.

*Adapted from John 8:12*

## Call

Let your steadfast love,
O LORD, be upon us,
**even as we hope in you.**

*Psalm 33:22*

## Psalm

*Read the Psalm of the day.*

### GLORIA IN EXCELSIS DEO

Glory to God in the highest and
peace to his people on earth.
Lord God, heavenly King,
Almighty God and Father,
we worship you, we give you thanks,
we praise you for your glory.
For you alone are the Holy One, you alone
are the Lord, you alone are the Most High,
Jesus Christ, with the Holy Spirit, in
the glory of God the Father. Amen.

## Adoration

### SILENCE OR SONG

*Seasonal song selections can be found on pp. 53–57.*

## Lesson

*Read the Old Testament passage of the day.*

## Prayer

My ego is like a fortress. I have built
its walls stone by stone to hold out the
invasion of the love of God. But I have
stayed here long enough. There is light over
the barriers. O my God—the darkness
of my house forgive, and overtake my
soul. I relax the barriers. I abandon all
that I think I am, all that I hope to be,
all that I believe I possess. I let go of
the past, I withdraw my grasping hand
from the future, and in the great silence
of this moment, I alertly rest my soul.

*A prayer of Howard Thurman (1899–1981), taken from All Will
Be Well. Thurman was an African American author, philosopher,
theologian, educator, and civil rights leader.*

## Abiding

### LECTIO DIVINA, VISIO DIVINA, OR PRAXIO DIVINA

*Pause at the end of this day. Enjoy communion with the living God:
Father, Son, and Holy Spirit. Listen for the voice of God in the
scriptures. Read. Meditate. Pray. Contemplate. Seek God's face.*

### INTERCESSORY PRAYER

Pray for the known needs of your
church, neighborhood, city, and world.

## Benediction

Finally, brothers and sisters, rejoice. Aim
for restoration, comfort one another, agree
with one another, live in peace; and may
the God of love and peace be with you.

*Adapted from 2 Corinthians 13:11*

**JAN 31**
NUM. 21
PS. 44
LUKE 3:21–38

**FEB 7**
NUM. 27
PS. 50
LUKE 5:27–32

**FEB 14**
NUM. 33
PS. 56
LUKE 7:11–17

**FEB 21**
DEUT. 3
PS. 62
LUKE 8:40–56

EVENING PRAYER

# WEDNESDAY

## Call

Rejoice in the Lord always;
**again I will say, rejoice.**

*Philippians 4:4*

## Psalm

*Read the Psalm of the day.*

### GLORIA IN EXCELSIS DEO

Glory to God in the highest and
peace to his people on earth.
Lord God, heavenly King,
Almighty God and Father,
we worship you, we give you thanks,
we praise you for your glory.
For you alone are the Holy One, you alone
are the Lord, you alone are the Most High,
Jesus Christ, with the Holy Spirit, in
the glory of God the Father. Amen.

**DEC 28**
ISA. 55
PS. 100
PHIL. 2:1-13

**JAN 4**
JOSH. 2:2-9
PS. 2
EPH. 6:10-20

**JAN 11**
NUM. 4
PS. 27
1 JOHN 4

**JAN 18**
NUM. 10
PS. 33
JAMES 2:1-13

## Adoration

### SILENCE OR SONG

*Seasonal song selections can be found on pp. 53–57.*

## Lesson

*Read the Old Testament passage of the day.*

## Prayer

**Confession:** We have been deceived;
Misguided by lies,
And disoriented by darkness.
In our error, correct us.
In our repentance, forgive us.
In our ignorance, illuminate us.
Jesus, your name is above every other name:
I worship you.

*Canyon Road: A Book of Prayer*

**Assurance:** And the Word became flesh
and dwelt among us, and we have seen
his glory, glory as of the only Son from
the Father, full of grace and truth.

*John 1:14*

## Abiding

### LECTIO DIVINA, VISIO DIVINA, OR PRAXIO DIVINA

*Pause at the start of a new day. Enjoy communion with the living God: Father, Son, and Holy Spirit. Listen for the voice of God in the scriptures. Read. Meditate. Pray. Contemplate. Seek God's face.*

### PROMPTED PRAYER

- For sanctification and growth in holiness
- For the opportunity and willingness to joyfully serve another person today
- For those who serve as missionaries from the East, West, North, or South

### THE LORD'S PRAYER

Our Father who art in heaven, hallowed
be thy name. Thy kingdom come, thy
will be done, on earth as it is in heaven.
Give us this day our daily bread; and forgive
us our debts, as we forgive our debtors;
And lead us not into temptation,
but deliver us from evil.
For thine is the kingdom and the
power and the glory, forever. Amen.

## Benediction

May the God of peace be
with you all. Amen.

*Romans 15:33*

## Call

Come to me, all who labor
and are heavy laden,
**and I will give you rest.**

*Matthew 11:28*

## Psalm

*Read the Psalm of the day.*

### GLORIA IN EXCELSIS DEO

Glory to God in the highest and
peace to his people on earth.
Lord God, heavenly King,
Almighty God and Father,
we worship you, we give you thanks,
we praise you for your glory.
For you alone are the Holy One, you alone
are the Lord, you alone are the Most High,
Jesus Christ, with the Holy Spirit, in
the glory of God the Father. Amen.

## Adoration

### SILENCE OR SONG

*Seasonal song selections can be found on pp. 53–57.*

## Lesson

*Read the New Testament passage of the day.*

## Prayer

You ask me where I get the joys that make
my heart so light, which all the gloom
of day destroys and gives me songs at
night. Hallelujah! I belong to the King.
I am saved now, and I have a right to
sing. For the light from heaven fills my
soul, and the night has passed away.

Adapted from the hymn "My Secret of Joy" by the Rev.
Dr. Charles Albert Tindley (1851–1933) of Philadelphia,
taken from *Songs of Zion.* Tindley is known as the "prince
of preachers" and a father of modern gospel music.

## Abiding

LECTIO DIVINA, VISIO DIVINA, OR PRAXIO
DIVINA

*Pause at the end of this day. Enjoy communion with the living
God: Father, Son, and Holy Spirit. Listen for the voice of God in
the scriptures. Read. Meditate. Pray. Contemplate. Seek God's face.*

PRAYER OF MINDFULNESS

*Throughout the history of the church, Christians have incor-
porated practices of prayer that call to mind God's presence in
the moment, humbly and gratefully review the time that has
passed, and look forward to the gift of another day. Pray through
these prompts slowly, giving time to each step of the practice.*

1. Become aware of God's presence.
2. Review the day with gratitude.
3. Pay attention to your emotions.
4. Choose one feature of the
   day and pray from it.
5. Look toward tomorrow.

## Benediction

The LORD bless you and keep you;
the LORD make his face to shine
upon you and be gracious to you;
the LORD lift up his countenance
upon you and give you peace.

*Numbers 6:24–26*

**JAN 25**
NUM. 16
PS. 39
JAMES 5:1-12

**FEB 1**
NUM. 22
PS. 45
LUKE 4:1-15

**FEB 8**
NUM. 28
PS. 51
LUKE 5:33-6:5

**FEB 15**
NUM. 34
PS. 57
LUKE 7:18-35

EVENING PRAYER

PRACTICES

# BEHOLD!

*Susan Porterfield Currie*

## MEDITATION

"Behold, the dwelling place of God is with man. He will dwell with them, and they will be his people, and God himself will be with them as their God."

—Revelation 21:3

Christmas and Epiphany—it is a time of the church year that invites us to engage all our senses in drawing near to God. Just notice the story of Jesus's birth: we experience scent (night air, animal dung, frankincense and myrrh), touch (straw rough underfoot, animal breath warm against skin), and sound (cows lowing, sheep bleating, and angel choirs singing, "Glory!").

And we are invited to *behold!* Immanuel, God-with-us, dwells among us, full of grace and truth. With Joseph and Mary, the shepherds and the wise men, Simeon and Anna, and the family of God through the ages and around the world, we come to the manger over the twelve days of Christmastide and gaze upon Christ Jesus in worship.

We continue our beholding during Epiphany. The word "Epiphany," in fact, means a manifestation, a revealing, and during the season of Epiphanytide we celebrate the revelation of Jesus to the world. Scripture readings during these weeks from the lectionary of the historic church begin with Jesus's visit by the wise men, then move to his baptism ("Behold, the Lamb of God!" John 1:29), on to the signs that begin with the wedding at Cana ("the first of the signs through which he revealed his glory," John 2:11), and culminating in his mountaintop Transfiguration, in which the disciples "saw his glory" (Luke 9:32).

This beholding represents the spiritual practice known as *visio divina*—literally "sacred vision," or what we might call holy looking, or holy gazing, that leads to deeper worship of and communion with God. We could say this holy looking begins in Genesis 1, with God himself being its first practitioner: "God saw all that he had made, and it was very good" (Gen. 1:31), and the implication of the following verses is that in gazing on creation's order and beauty and glory, God abided (his "rest" of the seventh day) in the midst of his own goodness.

ICELAND
*Jonatan Pie*

We see holy gazing later in Genesis, when God invites Abram to "look up at the sky and count the stars," and Abram believes God's promise (Gen. 15:5–6). And then of course David, the poet-shepherd-king, uses holy gazing as a prayer practice, allowing creation to reveal the presence and ways of God: "When I consider your heavens, the work of your fingers . . . ," he writes in Psalm 8 as he is led to worship, and in Psalm 19 he proclaims, "The heavens declare the glory of God; the skies proclaim the work of his hands. Day after day they pour forth speech; night after night they reveal knowledge."

It's important to distinguish between worshipping what we gaze on—that is idolatry, and it is soundly condemned throughout the scriptures—and letting what we gaze on be a window onto the presence and ways of God, who through Christ created all things (Heb. 1:2). When we practice visio divina, we do not pray *to* the objects or images of our attention; we merely let them open the eyes of our hearts to whatever God may want to reveal to us, through his Spirit in us, as we let our visual sense engage our spiritual senses.

Visio divina (sacred vision), much like lectio divina (sacred reading), may be explored through a four-stage process:

1.  visio (look on)
2.  meditatio (meditate or ruminate on, ponder)
3.  oratio (speak on, or discuss with God)
4.  contemplatio (simply rest in, in thankfulness)

Whether with a work of art or a view of nature outdoors, we begin simply by looking. As we look, we begin to notice what captures our attention (like the wise men, seeing the star in the sky), and we ponder it (like Mary, pondering "all these things" in her heart), and we let our pondering become a conversation with God (like Simeon, in his prayer as he held the infant Jesus), before finally coming to rest, becoming more deeply present to God with us (like the weaned child of Psalm 131, resting in its mother's arms, calmed and quieted and content).

Over time, as this spiritual practice becomes more natural and intuitive to us, the four stages will become more fluid and we'll find ourselves moving naturally between seeing and reflecting and praying and abiding in wonder, then praying some more and seeing some more and resting again in wonder and worship.

1. The art of Christmas and Epiphany offers a plentiful feast for the eyes. First, you'll need to choose an image to focus on. You can select one from the Gallery section of this periodical, or you might sit with a collection of Christmas cards you've received this year, or with a Nativity scene that's from your home or on public display in your area.

Gaze upon what draws your attention, then linger over the details—the colors, the movement, the textures and layers, the expressions, wherever your eyes are drawn or you notice your mind or your heart stirring.

Notice what goes through your mind, your heart, your imagination as you linger there. Let it become a conversation with God. What do you say to him? What does he say to you? Trust the Holy Spirit to lead your reflections and uncover deeper layers of awareness. What might be an accompanying invitation from God—something to be paying attention to, or to be praying, or to be doing?

Then rest in whatever the Lord speaks to you of his love. As you, through holy gazing, have communed with God, now let him gaze back upon you, in love. Keep his gaze.

Give the Lord thanks, and rest in his presence.

2. As we move through the winter months and the sensory fullness of Christmas and early Epiphany begins to fade, you may want to practice visio divina more broadly. Christ who fills all in all will meet you, through his indwelling Holy Spirit, in any pondering you engage in, but you may find it easiest to begin with objects or images that already have sacred meaning to you: a cross, the cup and plate of the Lord's Supper, a simple arrangement of a Bible and/or a lit candle on a table, a stained glass window, or some form of sacred art. You might stroll through an art museum prayerfully in conversation with the Lord as you notice what he draws your attention to and listen to why, and then let it become a doorway into communion, expressing glory.

3. Creation, the great artwork of our Creator, itself displays the glory of God. Practice visio divina with it—try both large-scale (a vista) and small (a pinecone dusted with snow, or the birds at your birdfeeder).

4. As this way of holy seeing becomes more natural to you, broaden your engagement even further.

How about gazing on those who bear the image of God—your fellow humans? Perhaps a sleeping baby, the eyes of a wise elder in the faith, the tired lines on the faces of those who step off the bus near your street corner . . . What conversation develops between you and the Lord as you do so?

How about photographs from the front page of the newspaper or from your online news feed? What is it to gaze on those and listen to the prayer that the Spirit shapes within you?

Susan Porterfield Currie (MATS, DMin, Gordon-Conwell Theological Seminary) is a minister for spiritual formation with Leadership Transformations, Inc., through which she founded and directs the Selah Certificate Program in Spiritual Direction. She and her husband, David, who is the dean of Gordon-Conwell's Doctor of Ministry program, serve as nonparochial clergy within the Anglican Church and are the parents of three adult children and a new grandchild (one of her own objects of *visio* beholding!). She writes for various curricular and devotional publications, including Selah's training curriculum.

*Pietro Ampazzo*

# MEDITATION FOR THE LIFE OF THE WORLD

*Russ Whitfield*

## MEDITATION

I really enjoy grocery shopping. I like to cruise through a freshly stocked produce section. I could spend long periods of time looking at all the different cuts of meat that they have on display. I like the surprise of discovering new food items that I can work into my repertoire because I also love to cook. But as much as I enjoy grocery shopping and as much as I love to cook, I love to eat so much more. In fact, the whole reason for grocery shopping and cooking is eating. You can grocery shop all day, but grocery shopping alone will not keep you alive. You can cook all day and smell the aromas, you can hear the sizzle, you can see a beautiful plate of food, but none of this can keep you alive if you don't sit down and eat. You won't have the nourishment you need to do anything else if you don't eat.

If you've been around the Christian faith for long, you have likely heard how central the Bible is to our life with God in the world. Many Christians enjoy studying the Bible. They read commentaries on scripture and study theological works about the Bible. They like to learn fun facts about the Bible that they didn't know before, and many can spend long periods of time in study. Studying the scriptures is like grocery shopping and cooking. But meditation is when we sit down and eat, and many Christians are malnourished because they have confused grocery shopping and cooking with eating. The purpose of spending time in study and growing in knowledge of the Christian faith is communion with God, and we will not have the nourishment we need to do anything else if we do not commune with him.

What does this meditation, this eating, look like? It is a sustained, imaginative reflection in which we listen for

God's voice in the scriptures with intent to be formed and to follow. It is considering his creation around us, his promises to us, and our future life with him—mindfully gazing on these and much more to be changed and oriented toward God. In other words, meditation is less like taking the mind of a scholar and more like taking the mind of a lover. It tunes our hearts to God's heart, keeping us grounded in him instead of in the superficialities of our age or the rush, hurry, and anxieties of our daily lives. Without eating, our bodies will quickly waste away. Without meditation, our souls will do the same. No one can eat for you, so take up meditation as a practice and may your delight increase in the Lord, and in that increase, may you bear much fruit for the life of the world.

## EXPLORATION

Consider how you can practice meditation in your daily and weekly life. Just as we make time to eat, set a place and a time. Protect it. Practice it. Your life, rootedness, fruitfulness, and resilience depend on it. Consider how you can practice meditation in the following areas:

1. *Meditate on the creation of God.* Cyril of Jordan said, "The wider our contemplation of creation, the grander is our conception of God." God has given the world around us as audio and visual elements to help expand the scope of our thinking and appreciation of him. Creation sings of God's glory, if we would listen. Meditation tunes our ears to the song.

2. *Meditate on the promises of God.* The scriptures are filled with God's promises—promises to be present with us, to provide for us, and his promise of a plan for our individual and communal lives. The more we meditate on the promises of God, the less we fall for the empty promises the world has to offer. These promises stabilize and energize us to live free of selfishness and self-interest for the interest of our neighbors.

3. *Meditate on our future with God.* One evening during family devotions, my children peppered me with questions about glory. "Will we be able to walk through walls like Jesus?" "What will it be like when sin doesn't exist?" "What does a new world look like?" I didn't have answers. We just meditated, and in that meditation, I began to long for glory. A feast is coming, but don't settle for the idea of the feast—picture it, smell it, taste it, feel it. Get it in your bones that there is joy to come, and watch that joy change you from the inside out.

Lastly, meditate on this: The good news from all eternity is that the Lord has been meditating on *you!* We've always been on his mind. David sings, "O Lord, what is man that you regard him, or the son of man that you think of him?" Can you fathom the truth that God has taken thought of you? May meditation on this truth enliven our imaginations and turn us into lovers who gaze at the one who looked upon us and loved us first. Look and live.

Russ Whitfield serves as pastor of Grace Mosaic, a cross-cultural church in Northeast Washington, DC. He is also the director of cross-cultural advancement for Reformed University Fellowship, a lecturer at Reformed Theological Seminary of Washington, DC, and the editor of the Daily Prayer Project.

GALLERY

"Behold, I bring you good tidings of great joy, *which shall be to all people*. For unto you is born this day in the city of David a Saviour, which is Christ the Lord."

—Luke 2:10–11 KJV, emphasis added

Jesus Christ was born for all people of all times. In light of this truth, artists around the globe have depicted him as coming into their own cultural contexts. The Italians and the Dutch did it during the Renaissance, setting events from the life of Christ in familiar landscapes populated by figures in local dress. So we shouldn't be surprised to find that artists from non-European countries sometimes visualize Jesus as incarnate in their own time and place, wearing *their* flesh, like a brother. The objection is sometimes made that to depict Jesus as anything other than a brown male born into a Jewish family in Bethlehem of Judea in the first century is to undermine his historicity. But the artists in this gallery aim, through their representational choices, to communicate theological meaning—picturing God's immanence, his "with-us-ness," and the universality of Christ's birth.

ETHIOPIA

## Mary with Christ Child

From an illuminated manuscript, 16th century
Collection of Na'akuto La'ab Monastery, near Lalibela
Photo: Alan Davey

# MORNING STAR

Born in Takaoka City, Hiroshi Tabata (1929–2014) studied art at the University of Toyama, later moving to France for two years for further art education. He exhibited his work throughout Japan and at Parisian salons. From 1966 to 1972 he lived intermittently in Brazil among the Xingu people, which led to his conversion to Christianity. From then on until his death, he painted biblical subjects. "The Bible is the ultimate theme for me," he said; its world is "infinitely deeper" than we can comprehend.

In Tabata's expressionistic *Morning Star,* starlight falls in a luminescent sheen over the face of the Christ child, whom Mary looks upon in tender adoration as Joseph wonders at the angelic activity above. The tight cropping around the Holy Family heightens the sense of intimacy. A sheep, donkey, and Amazon parrot (the latter a callback to his time in Brazil) crowd into the foreground, while on distant hills shepherds behold the glorious light display and hear the announcement that will propel them to their newborn Messiah. The wise men, too, are on their way. Epiphany is at hand. Heaven's raining down (Isa. 45:8).

JAPAN

## Morning Star
*Hiroshi Tabata, 1998*
Oil on canvas, 90.9 × 72.7 cm
Private collection

# IN BETHLEHEM

Balinese artist I Wayan Turun (1935–1986) from
Ubud shows the infant Christ lying down for a nap
under a bamboo lean-to in an Indonesian jungle.
Four agricultural laborers, wearing hats of woven
straw or coconut leaves, have come to see.

INDONESIA

## In Bethlehem
*I Wayan Turun, 1958*
Acrylic on canvas, 46 × 64 cm
Collection of Stichting
Zendingserfgoed, Zuidland,
Netherlands

# NATIVITY

Linda Syddick Napaltjarri (ca. 1937–2021) was a
Pintupi artist from Australia's Western Desert region
whose work was influenced by her Christian and
Indigenous beliefs and heritage. Adapting the traditional
visual language of her people, her *Nativity* tells the
story of Jesus's birth through wavy lines, minimalist
forms, and just a few colors. Mary, Jesus, and Joseph
are encompassed by concentric blue and white lines,
suggesting a sacramentality, while many more lines
converge on the trio from the image's border—or
alternatively, you could read these lines as radiating
outward. Jesus's birth both invites in and sends out.

AUSTRALIA

## Nativity
*Linda Syddick Napaltjarri, 2003*
Acrylic on linen, 94 × 121.9 cm
Private collection of Howard and
Roberta Ahmanson, Irvine, CA

# ADORATION OF THE CHRIST CHILD

Painted in an adapted Persian Islamic style in the Golconda kingdom of southern India, the anonymous *Adoration of the Christ Child* sets Jesus's birth in the court of Sultan Abdullah Qutb Shah (r. 1626–1672). Mary (wearing a nose ring!) and Joseph are flanked by attendants, and kneeling before the child is a Portuguese man who has traveled from afar, bearing gifts. Above, an angel descends with a flaming gold halo for the newborn prophet-king. Several Muslim rulers around that time—most famously Akbar the Great, the third Mughal emperor—were interested in interreligious dialogue, inviting Jesuits to court and encouraging their own court painters to visually interpret the sacred stories they told.

*Detail*

INDIA

## Adoration of the Christ Child
*Deccani School, ca. 1630*
Opaque watercolor and gold on paper, 15.6 × 11 cm
Collection of the Freer Gallery of Art,
Smithsonian Institution, Washington, DC

# NATIVITY

One of South Africa's most important printmakers, Azaria Mbatha (1941–2018) was a student and later teacher at the Evangelical Lutheran Art and Craft Centre at Rorke's Drift. In his Nativity linocut he shows a Nguni bull, two bushpigs, an elephant, and an antelope calf paying homage to the Christ child, whom a bald, long-bearded Joseph gestures toward. Three wise men approach on elephant-back from the left, and further to the left, King Herod lurks with lion and spear, waiting to pounce on this perceived threat to his power. The top two registers fast-forward to the beginnings of Jesus's public ministry, with John the Baptist preaching repentance and baptizing Jesus.

SOUTH AFRICA

## Nativity
*Azaria Mbatha, 1964*
Linocut, 33.5 × 57.5 cm

# NUEVO AMANECER

A Nativity image forms the backdrop of the activities of Centro Cultural Batahola Norte, a place of education, art and culture, recreation, and spiritual formation in Nicaragua's capital, founded to empower women and youth for social transformation. Painted in 1987 during the Nicaraguan Revolution, the *New Dawn* mural by the international artists' collective Boanerges Cerrato portrays Jesus surrounded by Latin American political revolutionaries Augusto C. Sandino, Che Guevara, Archbishop Óscar Romero, and Carlos Fonseca, as well as by women and children from the local community, who bring corn, cassava, bananas, watermelon, mangoes, papaya, pineapple, and other fruits of their harvest. By setting the birth amid Nicaraguans' decades-long struggle to liberate their country from both US imperialism and the repressive Somoza dictatorship, the mural is a reminder that Jesus came to free not just our souls but our whole selves, to promote justice and flourishing in *this* life as well as the next.

NICARAGUA

## Nuevo Amanecer (New Dawn)
*Boanerges Cerrato collective, 1987*
Mural, Centro Cultural Batahola Norte, Managua, Nicaragua

# ADORATION OF THE MAGI

Lastly, Daniel Bamidele, a Yoruba woodcarver from the Oye-Ekiti workshop in Nigeria, imagines Mary in a simple printed cloth dress and headwrap, supporting Jesus on her knee, a star hanging overhead. Joseph, holding a calabash of water, announces three visitors: Yoruba *oba* (kings) in traditional beaded *ade* (crowns), bringing carved vessels and a live chicken as gifts. These are the magi of Matthew's Gospel translated into an African context.

NIGERIA

## Adoration of the Magi
*Daniel Bamidele, ca. 1950*
Wood carving

# PRAYERS

THURSDAY MORNING TO SATURDAY EVENING

*Achmad al Fadhli*

# THURSDAY

## Call

Arise, shine, for your light has come, **and the glory of the LORD has risen upon you.**

*Isaiah 60:1*

## Psalm

*Read the Psalm of the day.*

### GLORIA IN EXCELSIS DEO

Glory to God in the highest and peace to his people on earth. Lord God, heavenly King, Almighty God and Father, we worship you, we give you thanks, we praise you for your glory. For you alone are the Holy One, you alone are the Lord, you alone are the Most High, Jesus Christ, with the Holy Spirit, in the glory of God the Father. Amen.

## Adoration

### SILENCE OR SONG

*Seasonal song selections can be found on pp. 53–57.*

## Lesson

*Read the New Testament passage of the day.*

## Prayer

Merciful and most loving God, by your will and mercy Jesus Christ our Lord humbled himself to exalt all humanity, and descended to the depths to lift up the lowly, and was born of a virgin, fully God and fully human, to restore in us your holy image that had been lost. Grant that your people may cling to you, that as you have redeemed us in your mercy, we may always please you by devoted service.

An ancient prayer taken from the Gallican Rite, a Latin

Christian liturgy translated from the Syriac-Greek rites of Jerusalem and Antioch in the early centuries of the church. Taken from *The New Ancient Collects.*

## Abiding

### LECTIO DIVINA, VISIO DIVINA, OR PRAXIO DIVINA

*Pause at the start of a new day. Enjoy communion with the living God: Father, Son, and Holy Spirit. Listen for the voice of God in the scriptures. Read. Meditate. Pray. Contemplate. Seek God's face.*

### PROMPTED PRAYER

- For the ability to see our own deficiencies and know the sufficiency of Jesus
- For the faithful witness of the church in your city and country
- For the poor and oppressed in your city

### THE LORD'S PRAYER

Our Father who art in heaven, hallowed be thy name. Thy kingdom come, thy will be done, on earth as it is in heaven. Give us this day our daily bread; and forgive us our debts, as we forgive our debtors; And lead us not into temptation, but deliver us from evil. For thine is the kingdom and the power and the glory, forever. Amen.

## Benediction

Hear the Lord say, "I am the light of the world. Whoever follows me will not walk in darkness, but will have the light of life." May you go from this place following after the Light of the World.

*Adapted from John 8:12*

MORNING PRAYER

## Call

Restore us, O God;
**let your face shine, that we may be saved!**
*Psalm 80:3*

## Psalm

Read the Psalm of the day.

### GLORIA IN EXCELSIS DEO

Glory to God in the highest and
peace to his people on earth.
Lord God, heavenly King,
Almighty God and Father,
we worship you, we give you thanks,
we praise you for your glory.
For you alone are the Holy One, you alone
are the Lord, you alone are the Most High,
Jesus Christ, with the Holy Spirit, in
the glory of God the Father. Amen.

## Adoration

SILENCE OR SONG

*Seasonal song selections can be found on pp. 53–57.*

## Lesson

*Read the Old Testament passage of the day.*

## Prayer

**Call:** Herod gave orders to kill all the boys
in Bethlehem and its neighborhood who
were two years old and younger. In this
way what the prophet Jeremiah had said
came true: "A sound is heard in Ramah,
the sound of bitter weeping. Rachel
is crying for her children; she refuses
to be comforted, for they are dead."

**Response:** Loving God, our hearts
are heavy with the sufferings of this
world. We remember the many victims
of political power and greed:
—the innocent killed in war and violence;
—all those who are tortured or put to death;
—those who languish in prison and camps;
—those missing or taken hostage;
—all whose lot your Son shared by
   being born when Herod was king.

**Lord, in your mercy, hear our prayer.**

*A responsive prayer taken from* With All God's People

## Abiding

LECTIO DIVINA, VISIO DIVINA, OR PRAXIO
DIVINA

*Pause at the end of this day. Enjoy communion with the living God:*
*Father, Son, and Holy Spirit. Listen for the voice of God in the*
*scriptures. Read. Meditate. Pray. Contemplate. Seek God's face.*

### INTERCESSORY PRAYER

Pray for the known needs of your
church, neighborhood, city, and world.

## Benediction

May the LORD answer you in the
day of trouble! May the name of
the God of Jacob protect you!
*Psalm 20:1*

EVENING PRAYER

# FRIDAY

## Call

And he came and preached peace
to you who were far off
and peace to those who were near.
**For through him we both have access in
one Spirit to the Father.**

*Ephesians 2:17–18*

## Psalm

*Read the Psalm of the day.*

GLORIA IN EXCELSIS DEO

Glory to God in the highest and
peace to his people on earth.
Lord God, heavenly King,
Almighty God and Father,
we worship you, we give you thanks,
we praise you for your glory.
For you alone are the Holy One, you alone
are the Lord, you alone are the Most High,
Jesus Christ, with the Holy Spirit, in
the glory of God the Father. Amen.

## Adoration

SILENCE OR SONG

*Seasonal song selections can be found on pp. 53–57.*

## Lesson

*Read the Old Testament passage of the day.*

## Prayer

O you who has given me eyes to see the
light that fills my room, give me the inward
vision to behold you in this place. O you
who has made me to feel the morning wind
upon my limbs, help me now to feel your
presence as I bow in the worship of you.

A prayer of Chandran Devansesen of India, adapted from
*Morning, Noon and Night.* Devanesen was a scholar and princi-
pal at Madras Christian College in Chennai.

### Sidebar calendar

**DEC 30**
ISA. 12
PS. 111
JAMES 3:13–18

*Epiphany of the Lord*
**JAN 6**
ISA. 60:1–6
PS. 72
MATT. 2:1–12;
EPH. 3:1–12

**JAN 13**
NUM. 6
PS. 29
2 JOHN

**JAN 20**
NUM. 12
PS. 35
JAMES 3:1–12

## Abiding

LECTIO DIVINA, VISIO DIVINA, OR PRAXIO
DIVINA

*Pause at the start of a new day. Enjoy communion with the living
God: Father, Son, and Holy Spirit. Listen for the voice of God in
the scriptures. Read. Meditate. Pray. Contemplate. Seek God's face.*

PROMPTED PRAYER

- For a heart that savors and
  shares the gospel of Christ
- For freedom from the love of money
  and for generosity in all of life
- For those who have been
  victims of a crime

THE LORD'S PRAYER

Our Father who art in heaven, hallowed
be thy name. Thy kingdom come, thy
will be done, on earth as it is in heaven.
Give us this day our daily bread; and forgive
us our debts, as we forgive our debtors;
And lead us not into temptation,
but deliver us from evil.
For thine is the kingdom and the
power and the glory, forever. Amen.

## Benediction

May the LORD keep your going
out and your coming in from this
time forth and forevermore.

*Psalm 121:8*

## Call

Yet God my King is from of old, working salvation in the midst of the earth.

**Yours is the day, yours also the night.**

*Psalm 74:12, 16a*

## Psalm

*Read the Psalm of the day.*

### GLORIA IN EXCELSIS DEO

Glory to God in the highest and peace to his people on earth. Lord God, heavenly King, Almighty God and Father, we worship you, we give you thanks, we praise you for your glory. For you alone are the Holy One, you alone are the Lord, you alone are the Most High, Jesus Christ, with the Holy Spirit, in the glory of God the Father. Amen.

## Adoration

### SILENCE OR SONG

*Seasonal song selections can be found on pp. 53–57.*

## Lesson

*Read the New Testament passage of the day.*

## Prayer

O Lord, we ask you to deliver us from fear of the unknown future, from fear of failure, from fear of poverty, from fear of sickness and pain, from fear of age, and from fear of death. Help us, O Father, by your grace to love and fear you only. Fill our hearts with cheerful courage and loving trust in you; through our Lord and Master Jesus Christ.

A prayer by Dr. Akanu Ibiam (1906–1995), a Nigerian medical missionary and governor

## Abiding

### LECTIO DIVINA, VISIO DIVINA, OR PRAXIO DIVINA

*Pause at the end of this day. Enjoy communion with the living God: Father, Son, and Holy Spirit. Listen for the voice of God in the scriptures. Read. Meditate. Pray. Contemplate. Seek God's face.*

### INTERCESSORY PRAYER

Pray for the known needs of your church, neighborhood, city, and world.

## Benediction

Now may our Lord Jesus Christ himself, and God our Father, who loved us and gave us eternal comfort and good hope through grace, comfort your hearts and establish them in every good work and word.

*2 Thessalonians 2:16–17*

**JAN 27**
NUM. 18
PS. 41
LUKE 2:21-40

**FEB 3**
NUM. 24
PS. 47
LUKE 4:31-44

**FEB 10**
NUM. 30
PS. 53
LUKE 6:12-23

**FEB 17**
NUM. 36
PS. 59
LUKE 8:1-15

EVENING PRAYER

# SATURDAY

## Call

The light shines in the darkness,
**and the darkness has not overcome it.**

*John 1:5*

## Psalm

*Read the Psalm of the day.*

### GLORIA IN EXCELSIS DEO

Glory to God in the highest and
peace to his people on earth.
Lord God, heavenly King,
Almighty God and Father,
we worship you, we give you thanks,
we praise you for your glory.
For you alone are the Holy One, you alone
are the Lord, you alone are the Most High,
Jesus Christ, with the Holy Spirit, in
the glory of God the Father. Amen.

## Adoration

### SILENCE OR SONG

*Seasonal song selections can be found on pp. 53–57.*

## Lesson

*Read the New Testament passage of the day.*

### CREED

Creo en un solo Señor, Jesucristo, Hijo
único de Dios, nacido del Padre antes
de todos los siglos: Dios de Dios, Luz
de Luz, Dios verdadero de Dios
verdadero, engendrado, no creado, de la
misma naturaleza del Padre, por quien todo
fue hecho; que por nosotros lo hombres, y
por nuestra salvación bajó del cielo, y
por obra del Espíritu Santo se encarnó
de María, la Virgen, y se hizo hombre.

We believe in one Lord, Jesus Christ, the
only Son of God, eternally begotten of
the Father, God from God, Light from
Light, true God from true God, begotten,
not made, of one Being with the Father.
Through him all things were made. For
us and for our salvation he came down
from heaven: by the power of the Holy
Spirit he became incarnate from the
Virgin Mary, and was made man.

*A portion of the Nicene Creed (382 CE)*

## Prayer

Dear Master, may your light shine on me
now, as it once shone upon the shepherds
as they kept their flocks by night.

*A prayer of Ozaki, a Japanese leprosy patient of the twentieth
century, adapted from Morning, Noon and Night. Throughout
the nineteenth and twentieth centuries, Christian ministers
and missionaries in Japan played a critical role in the care and
healing of leprosy patients.*

## Abiding

### LECTIO DIVINA, VISIO DIVINA, OR PRAXIO DIVINA

*Pause at the start of a new day. Enjoy communion with the living
God: Father, Son, and Holy Spirit. Listen for the voice of God in the
scriptures. Read. Meditate. Pray. Contemplate. Seek God's face.*

### PROMPTED PRAYER

- For a childlike rejoicing over
  the gracious gift of the Son
  of God, Christ Jesus
- For those who celebrate pregnancy
  or the birth or adoption of a child
- For the flourishing of all people in your
  place, from the womb to the tomb

### THE LORD'S PRAYER

*See p. 48 for text.*

## Benediction

May the steadfast love of the Lord be upon
us, even as we hope in him.

*Adapted from Psalm 33:22*

# SATURDAY

## Call

Let my prayer be counted
as incense before you,
**and the lifting up of my hands
as the evening sacrifice!**

*Psalm 141:2*

## Psalm

*Read the Psalm of the day.*

### GLORIA IN EXCELSIS DEO

Glory to God in the highest and
peace to his people on earth.
Lord God, heavenly King,
Almighty God and Father,
we worship you, we give you thanks,
we praise you for your glory.
For you alone are the Holy One, you alone
are the Lord, you alone are the Most High,
Jesus Christ, with the Holy Spirit, in
the glory of God the Father. Amen.

## Adoration

### SILENCE OR SONG

*Seasonal song selections can be found on pp. 53–57.*

## Lesson

*Read the Old Testament passage of the day.*

## Prayer

**Confession:** Lamb of God, you take away
the sins of the world, have mercy on us.
Lamb of God, you take away the sins
of the world, have mercy on us.
Lamb of God, you take away the sins
of the world, grant us peace.

*The Agnus Dei*

**Assurance:** Christ, our Passover lamb, has
been sacrificed. Let us therefore celebrate
the festival, not with the old leaven, the
leaven of malice and evil, but with the

unleavened bread of sincerity and truth.

*1 Corinthians 5:7–8*

## Abiding

### LECTIO DIVINA, VISIO DIVINA, OR PRAXIO DIVINA

*Pause at the end of this day. Enjoy communion with the living God: Father, Son, and Holy Spirit. Listen for the voice of God in the scriptures. Read. Meditate. Pray. Contemplate. Seek God's face.*

### PRAYER OF MINDFULNESS

1. Become aware of God's presence.
2. Review this past week with gratitude.
3. Pay attention to your emotions.
4. Choose one feature of the week and pray from it.
5. Look toward tomorrow and the beginning of a new week.

### A PRAYER FOR SABBATH

Creator God,
On the seventh day you rested
and were refreshed.
Please help me now to enter into
the rest of your Sabbath,
That I may cease from my work
And delight in your care over my life
Both now and forever,
Amen.

## Benediction

Lord, you now have set your servants free
to go in peace as you have promised, for
these eyes of ours have seen the savior,
whom you have prepared for all the world
to see: a light to enlighten the nations,
and the glory of your people Israel. Glory
to the Father, and to the Son, and to the
Holy Spirit: as it was in the beginning,
is now, and will be forever. Amen.

*The Nunc Dimittis (Song of Simeon), based on Luke 2:29–32*

EVENING PRAYER

David Beale

SONGBOOK

# SIZALELWE INDODANA

(UNTO US A CHILD IS BORN)

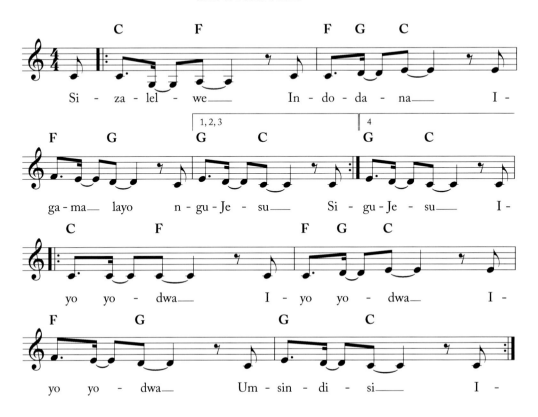

*English Translation*

Unto us a child is born
His name is Jesus
Only he is the Savior

Traditional South African Christmas song.

# O COME ALL YE FAITHFUL

1. O come, all ye faith - ful, joy - ful and tri -
2. Sing, choirs of an - gels, sing in ex - ul -
3. Yea, Lord, we greet thee, born this hap - py

um - phant! O come ye, O come— ye to Beth - le -
ta - tion,— sing, all ye ci - ti - zens of hea - v'n a -
mor - ning; Je - sus, to thee— be all glo - ry

hem! Come and be - hold him, born the King of an - gels.
bove! Glo - ry to God, all glo - ry in the high - est.
giv'n! Word of the Fa - ther, now in flesh ap - pea - ring.

O come, let us a - dore him,

O come, let us a - dore him,

O come, let us a - dore him,— Christ— the Lord!

Words: John Francis Wade; trans. Frederick Oakeley (1841; alt). Music: ADESTE FIDELES, John Francis Wade. Public domain.

# WALK IN THE LIGHT

Arrangement: Traditional African American. Words: James Vincent Coombs (1849–1920), refrain; Charles Wesley (1707–1788), verses; Anonymous, responses. Public domain.

# JESÚS ES MI LUZ Y MI SALVACIÓN

*English Translation*

The Lord is my light and my salvation, whom should I fear?
He is the strength of my life, the rock of salvation.
His justice shined on me. He placed my feet upon the rock. He lifted up my
head, my enemies he drove away. Praises to his name, I will sing.
Even though an army encamp against me, my heart will not fear; you will be there.
Although wars arise, although everyone surrounds me,
I'll trust you, yes, I'll trust you. I will trust in you.

Words and music by Coros Unidos, a Pentecostal Methodist music ministry of Santiago, Chile, © Coros Unidos.

Made in the USA
Middletown, DE
24 November 2022

15773995R00033